Good manners

This book belongs to

_____

Written by Stephen Barnett
Illustrated by Rosie Brooks

Contents

About this book

This book shows children the importance of good manners. It also shows them the need to be slow and steady in any work, and the need to respect everyone especially the elders in the family. Questions at the end test the child's attention and the section on new words helps in vocabulary building.

Good manners

John wanted to go for a movie.
He went to the living room
to ask his father to take him.

His father asked him what kind of a movie he would like to watch.

John told his father that he wanted to watch a movie about space and spaceships!

John's father agreed. But he
wanted John to use his manners
and be polite in his behaviour.

John could not understand how he could be polite while talking to his own dad!

John thought for a while. Then he
remembered that he needed to
say 'please' to his dad also.

So John asked his father again
if they could go for a movie. But
this time, with a 'please'.

John's father was glad. He told John that they could go for a movie right away!

John and his father rushed to a movie. John's father was happy as his son had learnt to be polite.

One step at a time

I wanted to play the flute well.
But I didn't think of practising. The
music sounded terrible when I
played.

I was unhappy. When my mother asked, I told her that playing the flute was very difficult!

My mother smiled and said that I needed to be patient and take one step at a time.

I listened to what she said and the next day I started playing the flute again.

For two weeks I practised a little bit each day, step by step as my mother had said.

After a month of practising I was
playing better than before. And I
was enjoying it too!

Now I play quite well. Dad says that I could try to improve my mathematics as well, step by step!

Respect

One day, my grandparents came
to have dinner with us. When
they arrived, my parents took
great care of them.

Our mother always told us that we should respect everyone, especially your parents and grandparents.

My brother and I sat down next
to our grandparents and told
them what we learnt at school.

Then we helped to set the table
and bring out the food for the
meal.

At dinner we listened to what our grandparents had to say and served them when they wanted more food.

Later, we helped to clear the table, to wash and dry the dishes as well.

When our grandparents were
leaving, my brother
and I ran to the door to say
goodbye.

After our grandparents left, we
said goodnight to our parents.

One day when I grow old, I hope younger people will have respect for me for what I have done.

New words

movie
living room
manners
watch
space
spaceship
agreed
polite
behaviour
understand
needed
remembered
thought
please
talking
glad
rushed
learnt
flute
practising
played
music
sounded
terrible

unhappy
difficult
smiled
patient
listened
started
month
enjoying
better
improve
mathematics
arrived
great
dinner
always
respect
especially
school
served
helped
clear
goodbye
goodnight

What did you learn?

Good manners
Where did John want to go?
What was the word John needed to say to his father?

One step at a time
Why was the child unhappy?
What did her mother tell her to do?
Did it help her?

Respect
Who was coming to dinner?
How did the children help?
What did you learn from the story?